Security and Surveillance DRONES

Leanne Currie-McGhee

ReferencePoint Press

San Diego, CA

About the Author

Leanne Currie-McGhee lives in Norfolk, Virginia, with her husband, Keith, daughters, Grace and Hope, and dog, Delilah. She has written educational books for over eighteen years.

© 2021 ReferencePoint Press, Inc.
Printed in the United States

For more information, contact:
ReferencePoint Press, Inc.
PO Box 27779
San Diego, CA 92198
www.ReferencePointPress.com

LIBRARY OF CONGRESS CATALOGING-IN-PUBLICATION DATA

Names: Currie-McGhee, Leanne, author.
Title: Security and surveillance drones / by Leanne Currie-McGhee.
Description: San Diego, CA : ReferencePoint Press, [2021] | Series: World
  of drones | Includes bibliographical references and index.
Identifiers: LCCN 2020003121 (print) | LCCN 2020003122 (ebook) | ISBN
  9781682828373 (library binding) | ISBN 9781682828380 (ebook)
Subjects: LCSH: Crime prevention--Juvenile literature. | Drone
  aircraft--Juvenile literature. | Search and rescue operations--Equipment
  and supplies--Juvenile literature. | Police--Equipment and
  supplies--Juvenile literature. | Border patrols--Equipment and
  supplies--Juvenile literature.
Classification: LCC HV7431 .C865 2021 (print) | LCC HV7431 (ebook) | DDC
  364.4028/4--dc23
LC record available at https://lccn.loc.gov/2020003121
LC ebook record available at https://lccn.loc.gov/2020003122

CONTENTS

INTRODUCTION

Tools of Surveillance and Security

Since 2018 a drone—an unmanned aerial vehicle—has zoomed through the skies of Ensenada, Mexico. This drone, the Inspire 1, is a quadcopter, a drone with four arms, each of which has a propeller used to lift it into the air. The Inspire 1 is just over 6 pounds (2.7 kg), has a max speed of 49 miles per hour (79 kph), can stay aloft up to eighteen minutes, and is able to transmit video from up to 3.1 miles (5 km) away from the operator. The Mexican police force in Ensenada has used the Inspire 1 as part of its crime control mission. The authorities claim that it has led to more than five hundred arrests, a 10 percent reduction in the overall crime rates and a 30 percent drop in home robberies since it became a part of the force.

During a four-month period, the police department flew the Inspire 1 on an average of twenty-five missions a day. Controlling the drone from the station, the officers piloted the drone to locations in response to 911 calls. From their control room, the police used software to oversee the movements of the drone while watching the video feed from the drone. At their desks, or even in the field, officers could use a smartphone to view the video from the drone and respond to any illegal activity captured. "It's helped with reducing response times and also catching people when they do something illegal,"[1] says chief technology officer Jesus Ramos Avendaño. He attributes the crime drop to the increased ability of officers to rapidly respond to situations. Similarly, other police forces around the world are using drones regularly to assist in all types of missions, including locating elusive suspects and engaging in search and rescue operations.

Police are not the only people using drones for search and rescue, however. On the evening of October 15, 2019, Ethan Haus, a six-year-old, went missing in Remington, Minnesota, after going outside to play with his dog. Six hundred volunteers turned out to search for him, but it was a drone that found him.

Steve Fines, who owns a drone imaging company, was one of the search party volunteers. He decided to bring a drone with a thermal camera on the search. He deployed his drone, and in the early morning of October 16, the drone captured a thermal picture of Ethan and the dog in a cornfield east of the family's home. This was an area that volunteers had not yet searched. After receiving the picture, Fines informed the authorities, who responded to the location and found the boy. "If not for that drone, I'm not sure we would have found him,"[2] Sherburne County sheriff Joel Brott says. Search and rescue missions in the United States and other countries have experienced similar successes when using drones to assist them.

elusive

Difficult to catch

Law enforcement agencies worldwide are using drones (such as this quadcopter) to assist with all types of cases. Drones are easily deployed and able to cover large areas relatively quickly.

Technical Advantages of Drones

What made Fines's drone so effective in finding Ethan and the police drones in performing surveillance is that they can easily deploy and cover a large area in a short amount of time. All drones are either fixed-wing craft, for which lift is generated by the wings, like an airplane, or craft that are rotor powered like a helicopter. Fixed-wing drones are generally larger and less easy to transport than rotor drones, but they can fly over larger areas for a longer time. Conversely, rotor drones require less space to take flight, can hover in an area to inspect it, and can maneuver quickly. Although there are different types and sizes of drones, all drones are made with light composite materials to increase maneuverability while flying and reduce weight, allowing them to fly rapidly and stay in the air longer.

Moving swiftly and staying aloft for up to thirty minutes on a single battery charge gives drones a good range. This, coupled with an onboard camera, permits drones and their users to investigate large areas from high above. The pictures that Fines's drone transmitted to him, for example, allowed him to actually see, in real time, a much larger area than he could have covered on foot. Additionally, the drone camera's thermal ability was key for locating the lost boy. Thermal cameras are programmed to recognize and capture different levels of infrared light produced by heat. The camera detects the heat and assigns each level of heat a shade of color, which can be seen in the transmitted images. So while it may have been difficult to see Ethan in a regular photo because of the foliage around him or darkness, a thermal image revealed the heat he emitted.

Whereas Fines's drone was equipped with a thermal camera, there are several other technical features that drones can have to add to their abilities, making them useful to search and rescue, security, and surveillance missions. Drones can be equipped with high-definition cameras and video recorders, navigation systems, and heat sensors. Additionally, while many drones are operated in real time by a pilot on the ground, drones can fly autonomously.

That is, they can be preprogrammed to completely fly a mission on their own, taking pictures and returning to their base on a specified schedule. Some drones can also be programmed to automatically follow a moving target while avoiding collisions with any obstacles along the way. Such abilities require artificial intelligence, and advances in this field are providing drone imaging technology with the ability to read license plates or recognize specific human faces.

Increasing Use

The uses of drones are increasing as more people and organizations understand their capabilities. According to its *Security Drones Report 2017*, IFSEC Global, a provider of news and research on security, found that of the security agencies in its survey, 60 percent either already used drones or could foresee themselves doing so eventually. Additionally, the Center for the Study of the Drone at Bard College reported that as of May 2018, 910 US state and local public safety agencies actively used drones to fight crime and protect communities. Ultimately, whether searching for a person in danger or scanning for a crime in action, drones are becoming an often-used tool for security and surveillance because they can be activated quickly and give the operators an immediate picture of an area under observation. As John Noland, a lieutenant with the Santa Rosa Police Department in California, states, "It's 50 times quicker than you could put people on horseback, motorcycles, bikes, or on foot. It gives you real-time intelligence."[3] For these reasons, drones are likely to remain in security service for years to come.

CHAPTER 1

Search and Rescue

In 2016 a man's car flipped over on an isolated road in Grimsby, United Kingdom, during the early morning hours. Witnesses saw him wandering after the accident, and he was apparently disoriented. When the Lincolnshire Police arrived, the man could not be found. The evening was freezing cold, and the authorities were worried that he could die of hypothermia if not found quickly. The police decided to deploy their drone, which had thermal imaging, while other officers searched on foot. Within a few minutes, the drone located the man. He was unconscious in a 6-foot-deep (1.8 m) ditch, several feet off the main road. Without the drone, the police would have been searching the road and fields in the hours before the sun rose, and the man could have died if he went unseen in the dark.

The Lincolnshire Police is one of many organizations around the world that are discovering the usefulness of drones in search and rescue. According to report by DJI, a drone manufacturer, from May 2017 to April 2018, sixty-five people were rescued worldwide due to drone surveillance in search and rescue missions. As more rescue organizations obtain drones, the company predicts this number will rise.

Who Uses Drones for Search and Rescue?

Emergency services, such as fire and police departments, are the most common organizations employing drones to assist with locating lost people. These agencies are acquiring drones and training their officers in how to use them. Then the agencies employ the drones as a part of their regular operations during search and rescue.

Other groups employing drones are those that must prepare for emergency situations that routinely result in search and rescue operations. Mountain rescue units, national and state park agencies, and lifeguards often stage such operations because of the nature of their services. As an example, the Czech Mountain Rescue Service uses Robodrone Kingfisher drones—fitted with six rotors, cameras, and avalanche transceiver detection systems—to locate skiers buried in avalanches. All skiers in seven different districts served by the Mountain Rescue Service are provided transceivers, hand-sized radio devices that emit a low-power pulsed signal when activated. If skiers are in an avalanche or lost, they can activate their transceiver's signal. The drones can then detect the skiers, following the signal.

transceivers

Hand-sized radio devices that emit a low-power pulsed signal when activated

Civilian groups are also using drones to assist with finding people, and some have developed their own organizations. Texas EquuSearch is an all-volunteer organization developed to assist local law enforcement personnel in searching for missing persons. This organization started in the Houston region and has opened chapters around the nation since its inception. Texas EquuSearch implemented drones as a part of its operations in 2014.

Deploying Drones to Search in Difficult Terrain

The most common use of search and rescue drones is to locate individuals who have become lost in areas such as a forest or mountains, where ground search can be slow and difficult. Drones have found hikers stranded in the wilderness, individuals trapped by volcanic eruptions and earthquakes, and even swimmers lost at sea.

The National Park Service of the Grand Canyon implemented a drone program in 2016 with five drones and four certified operators to assist in all types of searches. The drones they use are about 18 inches (46 cm) wide and 10 inches (25 cm) high, and they have a battery life of about twenty minutes. The drones routinely scan the park for signs of visitors in trouble. Drone operators scrutinize video footage from the drone in real time, and analyze it again at the end of the day to make sure they have not missed any details. In some cases, the drones are used to find individuals who are beyond help. For example, in December 2016 a woman deliberately jumped to her death in the canyon. The drones were deployed, and review of the feed pinpointed her location, allowing rangers to rappel down to retrieve the body.

Drones are particularly useful for search and rescue missions in rugged or heavily forested terrain.

Fighting Fire with Fire

Firefighters already use drones to provide high-altitude images to chart the paths of wildfires. More recently, drones have been developed that can actually fight fires by starting control fires. These drones carry plastic spheres filled with a flame accelerant called potassium permanganate. The Ping-Pong-ball-size spheres are injected with glycol right before being dropped. The glycol reacts with the potassium permanganate, which creates flames in less than thirty seconds. These controlled fires burn out areas of undergrowth so that raging wildfires moving into those areas will have no new fuel to consume, stopping the fires in their tracks. This helps firefighters contain the advance of wildfires and direct them away from homes and businesses. The first drones with this system were developed by a team at the University of Nebraska, and now a private company named Drone Amplified, in partnership with the US Department of the Interior, offers drones equipped with this helpful technology.

The drones reduce the dangers for park service employees as well. In the past, rangers would have to employ helicopters on searches, and flying through crevices and tight spaces is dangerous. "Our historic model was to take the helicopter to look and see," says Grand Canyon chief ranger Matt Vandzura. "[But drones provide] that same close look but without putting any people at risk. It has dramatically increased our ability to keep our people safe."[4]

Drones Speed Rescues

Drones can keep searchers safe and speed the rescue of those who are in peril. The Lochaber Mountain Rescue Team, located in the Highlands of Scotland, has employed drones for several years to assist in finding lost climbers and hikers in the mountains. Snow and freezing temperatures in the Highlands make it essential to find people quickly when they are lost or injured. In July 2017 a female climber injured her leg while climbing in the region. The Lochaber team piloted its drone over the area to take photographs and create a 3-D image of the area, which quickly led the team to the climber. The drone helped search the large area efficiently and expeditiously. It also allowed the team the ability to search remote areas that are difficult to traverse. "I would say that using a drone makes it 50% quicker than traditional methods to do a search," explains Mike Smith, a Lochaber crew member. "It widens the search area for us, allowing us to get an overview of the area—how big it is and inspect areas of concern, such as cornices (an overhanging ledge of snow), which can be 40ft long."[5] As of 2017 Lochaber had two members trained to pilot drone rescue missions, and the unit planned to expand the training on the basis of its successes with its drones.

Natural disasters such as earthquakes and volcanic eruptions are other emergency situations in which drones can assist those lost or stuck in a place. After the Kilauea volcano erupted on Hawaii's Big Island in May 2018, the US Geological Survey deployed a drone to locate a trapped man. He had called emergency services when his residence was surrounded by lava. The drone was flown to his home, and it located him by spotting the flashlight on his cell phone. It was too dangerous for the rescue team to attempt to get to his home, but the information the drone provided allowed the team to help him. The live footage from the drone showed the areas surrounding the man, allowing the rescue group to determine the safest escape route for him. While talking to the man on his cell phone, the team used the drone's visual information to direct him out of his home and toward a safe area. The drone followed him as he escaped the lava, and the team continued to direct his path until he was safe.

Drones Can Carry Rescue Devices

Providing assistance to those in danger is not typically thought of as a role for drones, but it is becoming more common. Lifeguards in Australia, for example, are able not only to find struggling swimmers via drones but also to provide them material assistance. In 2018 two teenage boys were swimming off the shore of New South Wales when they began to struggle in the current.

Drones can deliver flotation devices to individuals who find themselves unable to swim to shore on their own.

People noticed them and notified the lifeguards. Immediately, the lifeguards deployed a drone, which spotted them a half mile (805 m) from the beach. After piloting the drone toward the boys, the controllers had the drone drop them a yellow flotation device. The device inflated once in the water, and the boys were able use it to get to safety. For the drone to locate the boys and provide the flotation device took only seventy seconds, rather than the six minutes it typically takes lifeguards to traverse the same distance.

The company Little Ripper Lifesaver, which developed the drone, develops and integrates lifesaving devices into lightweight pods that can be carried and deployed by drones. The company has also developed pods that can carry automated external defibrillators, electromagnetic shark repellant devices, and personal survival kits (which include water, a thermal blanket, a radio, and a first aid kit). Local governments throughout Australia are employing these drones as part of their lifeguard rescue services as the manufacturer continues to develop new uses.

defibrillators

Devices that restore a normal heartbeat by sending an electric pulse or shock to the heart

Drones Can Help Assess Emergency Situations

Besides locating individuals and transporting lifesaving equipment, drones are also used to help authorities assess emergency situations before response measures are taken. Fire departments have found that drones can provide needed intelligence on how to fight fires. Departments on the West Coast of the United States use drones when assessing wildfires to protect their firefighters from harm. Plane and helicopter crashes accounted for 24 percent of wildland firefighter deaths from 2006 to 2016, according to the US Forest Service. For this reason responders are turning to drones to accomplish some of their tasks. Drones can be equipped with infrared cameras that allow them to see through smoke and with sensors that detect wind direction and other weather variables that affect how wildfires spread. This lets firefighters predict the route of a wildfire and gives them the ability to warn people who might need to escape the oncoming flames.

In 2018 nearly four thousand firefighters were battling the Ferguson Fire in California, which was so widespread and fast moving that the thousands of firefighters could not keep track of its path. For this reason, they deployed drones provided by the California Air National Guard to locate hot spots that needed immediate attention. "To have a platform that can see through smoke and actually go around the fire and pick those spots out and be able to communicate that back down to the ground and

Drones can provide critical information such as wind speed and direction to wildland firefighters, to keep them safer.

back up to us, so that way we can mitigate the spots is game changing,"[6] situation unit leader Damian Guilliani says. The Air National Guard drones were able to collect data, transmit it to the firefighting crews who interpreted the videos and pictures, and then determine where to go to fight the fires and save people. Ultimately, the drones helped them rescue those in danger while reducing the danger to themselves.

Drone Efficiency Study Results

Because of their usefulness, drones will likely become an integral part of more search and rescue teams. The 2018 Drone Efficacy Study, conducted by DJI, the European Emergency Number Association (EENA), and Black Channel (an Irish research group), has helped organizations see how useful drones can be in search and rescue operations. The study researched the effectiveness of drones in these operations and how drone-equipped teams perform in comparison to ground-only teams.

Monitoring Sharks in Coastal Waters

As Australia has turned to drones to assist swimmers struggling at sea, it also has discovered that drones are effective at helping people avoid shark attacks. In 2017 Australia added drones to its lifeguard fleets to assist with shark detection in coastal waters. The drones are equipped with shark-spotting software that can identify sharks from the images received through the onboard camera. Nabin Sharma, a research associate at the University of Sydney's Technology School of Software, explains that the drones help improve the accuracy of aerial shark detection, because humans are only able to visually identify sharks with 20 to 30 percent accuracy when analyzing aerial imagery. The software system equipped on the drones can detect sharks with 90 percent accuracy. This allows the lifeguard fleets to monitor shark movements near waters that might be shared by human swimmers.

For the study, thirty teams used drones with standard visual cameras, while another twenty teams searched on foot without drones. Seventeen (85 percent) of the ground teams found the victims in the simulated search and rescue operations, while twenty-three (roughly 76 percent) of the drone teams accomplished the task. However, of the teams that found the victims, the study revealed that searchers using drones found their targets an average of 191 seconds—or more than three minutes—faster than the ground teams. Even though a higher percentage of teams without drones found their victims, the study concluded that the poorer showing from drone users was due to a lack of understanding of how best to use the drones. The researchers emphasized the necessity of training rescue teams in the best methods of drone use. Alfonso Zamarro, EENA drones activities manager, says:

Searchers in the study said finding a victim with a drone was harder than they expected, which shows why it is vital for the [search and rescue] community to develop best standards for how to use drones. What patterns should drones fly? What altitude provides the best coverage? What sensors are best for spotting missing people? Which areas are best searched by ground forces, and which by drones? Answering these questions won't be easy, but it will have a powerful impact.[7]

Such research will likely drive search and rescue organizations to adopt drone technology. Given the correct training and the funds to acquire drones with the right features, search and rescue teams will add powerful tools to their arsenals. With these, rescuers will expand their capabilities and increase the success of their operations.

CHAPTER 2

Law Enforcement Use

While many public safety agencies have found drones useful in search and rescue missions, law enforcement agencies have discovered that drones can assist them in many other ways. Drones assist law enforcement with locating suspects, assessing dangerous situations, and more. As of May 2018, 910 US state and local public safety agencies employed drones for both surveillance and security to achieve their mission of fighting crime and protecting the populace.

Locating Suspects

A primary use of drones by police forces is to search for crime suspects. Police forces are discovering that in certain situations it is cheaper to use a drone to follow a suspect who is trying to get away. "It took a helicopter to chase bad guys in the past, and it was very expensive to do that—something that an agency our size could never possibly afford,"[8] says Lieutenant Russell Brown of the Bellaire Police Department in Texas. Now the department can choose to use a drone. The drones are capable of flying at 50 miles an hour (80 kph), have a range of about 3 miles (5 km), and can rise to 400 feet (122 m). Additionally, they are equipped with thermal cameras that can zoom in to locate suspects who are attempting to hide. The Bellaire Police Department has three drones and four licensed drone pilots.

In 2019 a burglary suspect was fleeing, and officer Aaron Lysack, one of the department's licensed drone pilots, received a call to assist with locating the suspect. Lysack was patrolling in his police cruiser at the time. He simply stopped driving and sent the drone into the air to aid the search. The drone flew in the area surrounding the site of the burglary and located the suspect before the officers could. Once the suspect was spotted, the officers closed in. The drone also recorded the suspect attempting to throw a backpack away. When the officers arrived, they apprehended the suspect and got the backpack, which was filled with stolen items and a gun. "The drone was able to see that, document that on film, and have that video ready for court if needed,"[9] Brown says.

First on the Scene

The Chula Vista, California, police force has found similar uses for drones. In 2019, less than a year after it launched its first drone, the department was celebrating its one thousandth flight. By that point, drones had helped in 130 arrests. One reason for this, according to the department, is that drones are able to get to

Many police departments have begun using drones instead of costly helicopters to search for criminal suspects.

a crime scene in about two minutes, while it takes a patrol unit closer to six minutes.

When drones are used by the department, the process usually works something like this: A call comes in and an officer determines that a drone could be helpful on this call. An officer who is trained to work with drones programs into it the geo-fence, a virtual geographic boundary set by GPS, to tell the drone what area to search. An officer on the roof launches the drone and has the ability to override the settings if an obstruction, like a flock of birds or manned aircraft, interferes with the search pattern. Federal law allows drones to be flown only within the operator's line of sight, so the officer on the roof must be able to see the drone. During one of these operations in 2019, a woman motorist was ramming her car into a man on a motorcycle and chasing him down the streets of Chula Vista. A police drone was flown after them, and as it tracked the woman, it broadcast a live video feed to patrol officers' smartphones. Because of the drone footage, officers knew the nature of the incident and where to find the woman. Thanks to the evidence provided by the drone, upon arriving on the scene, the officers immediately arrested the woman for assault.

Crime Scene Investigation

Drones are often used to capture pictures and video to assist law enforcement in solving crimes. As with the Chula Vista example, such images can be used as evidence in court. And because drones can take pictures from great altitudes, they can provide images of crime scenes that might not be easily obtained otherwise.

In Mesa County, Colorado, the sheriff's department uses a drone to take multiple photos in a grid pattern at a specific crime scene. These photos give the department enough information to re-create a scene in three dimensions. Such detailed mapping is called Orthographic Mosaic Imaging, or orthomosaics. In the past, the sheriff's department had to rely on helicopters to get photos from above, which is costly. The department found that using drones to take photographs costs only twenty-five dollars an hour. From a ground control station, the drone operator will program the drone to select an area to photograph and will specify how many photos to take. The drone will then calculate the grid and fly on its own. The drone flies above the scene at an altitude of roughly 50 feet (15 m). Using a twenty-megapixel camera, the drone can capture photos so sharp they can be enlarged to nearly life size. Once the photos are taken, the images can be used to create a 3-D replica of the area due to overlap and angles in the pictures

Major Investment in Drones

The government of The Bahamas is so convinced that drones will pay off in the fight against crime that it has spent a lot of money to acquire a fleet of them. In 2019 the Bahamian minister of national security, Marvin Dames, signed a $17 million contract with California-based Swift Systems to develop a multiagency drone program. This is to be used across law enforcement agencies to assist in combating the smuggling of migrants, drugs, firearms, and more. According to Dames:

> This contract is for about $17m and it's for 55 short and medium range drones—we did that purposely because . . . it will allow for us to accommodate all the law enforcement agencies. That is the Royal Bahamas Police Force, the Royal Bahamas Defense Force, Bahamas Department of Corrections. We also have the immigration, customs and as well as the other government ministries. It is expected that these drones will be used throughout the length and breadth of this country.

> The contract includes not only the purchase of the drones but the training of officers to use them in situations such as following robbery suspects, locating illegal immigrants, monitoring prisons, or spotting drug boats. Dames expects the program to significantly reduce crime in his nation.

Quoted in Syann Thompson, "17 M Drone Deal Takes Crime Fight to the Sky," *Tribune* (Nassau, Bahamas), December 17, 2019. www.tribune242.com.

taken. The detail allows investigators to simulate possible events that led up to a crime, locate geographic relationships between individuals involved, and plot how the crime unfolded. The orthomosaics are as admissible in court like any other method of crime scene reconstruction and can be used to help convict a criminal. According to Ben Miller, Mesa County's unmanned aircraft program director at the sheriff's of-

orthomosaic model

A detailed, accurate photo representation of an area, created out of many aerial photos that have been stitched together and corrected to scale

fice, orthomosaic models have assisted in the outcome of one court case and are involved in several ongoing ones.

Traffic Surveillance

While finding criminals and reconstructing crime scenes are important, drones are also helpful to law enforcement in other instances. For one, drones are helpful in overseeing traffic and spotting traffic offenders. London, England, for example, has deployed drones to help reduce vehicle accident deaths due to mo-

Authorities in the United Kingdom have begun using drones to patrol rush hour roadways in search of motorists who are speeding or driving recklessly.

Training Drone Operators

To be effective, drones need operators who can use them properly. Law enforcement agencies that have obtained drones have found that they must train officers to use them. These officers must learn the laws pertaining to drones. The Federal Aviation Administration (FAA), a governmental body of the United States that regulates civil aviation in the nation, establishes rules for drone use, and law enforcement is bound by those rules. One such requirement is for an agency to obtain a certificate of authorization from the FAA to operate a drone. Then officers need to learn how to safely fly the drone and must understand its features. They also must pass a test to obtain a Remote Pilot Certificate from the FAA. That exam covers airspace classification and operating requirements, as well as flight restrictions affecting small unmanned aircraft operation, knowledge of weather effects on small unmanned aircraft performance, proper loading and performance of small unmanned aircraft, and emergency procedures. Many agencies send their officers to training courses offered by commercial organizations, but others do in-house training.

torists driving recklessly and disobeying traffic rules. The drones are deployed to survey the roads where dangerous driving, such as speeding, has commonly occurred. Once the drone spots a suspect, it relays information from the drone to police officers who are out patrolling. The officers then rush to the scene and pull the offender over. This is done both day and night, since the drone has a night vision camera.

London's Metropolitan Police Service believes that seeing drones patrolling the air also deters drivers from breaking laws. According to Detective Superintendent Andy Cox, head of the Metropolitan's roads and traffic policing unit, "The focus [of drones] will be on dangerous drivers who are racing and those putting their lives and other people's at risk. However, deterrence is sometimes best achieved through intense enforcement and that's what this capability enables."[10]

Monitoring Protests

Some law enforcement agencies also use drones to monitor protests, in which people gather to voice their opposition to an existing or proposed law or action. In New Delhi, India, for example, citizens gathered in the streets in 2019 to protest a new law. Police used drones with thermal imaging—that could fly as high as 656 feet (200 m) and scan an area of up to 2.5 miles (4 km)—to take photographs and videos of the people on the streets. The drones were used to record the event in case protestors or any member of the public committed violence, property damage, or other crime in such a tense situation.

Taking the use further, in Israel police have used drones to break up crowds of protesters at the Gaza border. Tens of thousands of Gazans marched in the streets in 2018, calling for Palestinians to be allowed to return to the land that their ancestors fled during the 1948 Arab-Israeli War. Israeli border police used drones to drop canisters of tear gas on the protesters to disperse the gatherings.

Police in India are using drones to monitor street protests. Surveillance of this kind is controversial in the United States.

Using drones in these situations is controversial among law enforcement agencies in many countries. In the United States drone use at protests has been considered by police, but it has not become the norm. While drones have been flown in California at some protests, most states have not used them regularly for this purpose. Authorities are reluctant to do so, since many citizens in the United States believe it violates their privacy rights.

Assessing Danger

As with protests, drones can be used in other ways to assess danger in order to limit the threat that a police officer might face. Agencies have found drones to be beneficial in assessing bomb threats or the capabilities of armed suspects. When a threat is made, police have found that they can use drones to help assess the situation and make a decision on how to respond.

In 2019 the police department in Daytona Beach, Florida, used a drone from its Unmanned Aviation Unit after a man threatened to set off a grenade in a hotel room. Emergency dispatchers received a call indicating that a man was making threats to kill himself on the fifth floor of the Ocean Breeze Club Hotel and would detonate a grenade if police tried to enter his room. The hotel was evacuated, and the Unmanned Aviation Unit flew a drone outside the hotel room's patio window to assess the threat. After viewing the footage the drone took, police officers determined that the grenade was not operational. The drone gave them vital information that helped them make a decision on how to deal with the suspect. Officers eventually took the man into custody after luring him out of his room, and no one was harmed in the process.

Across the country, in Pittsburg, California, a man suspected of firing shots at his family barricaded himself inside his home. Family members had come to see him and were approaching the house when he discharged one of his two handguns. No one was injured, and they called the authorities. He then barricaded himself inside, refusing to come out when ordered to do so by the police. Police officers employed a drone with high-definition video to review the situation, which reduced the danger to the officers and gave them the information needed for proceeding. "We were able to use the drones to determine where the doors and windows were in the backyard to relay that to the SWAT team so they could make decisions about how they were going to do the SWAT operation,"[11] says Detective Nicholas Law, who heads the unmanned aerial vehicle program. Law says that with the drone, the officers could ensure that the man was not trying to escape from another area of the house. The suspect eventually walked out of his home after five hours and was taken into custody.

Newest Implementations

As the technology of drones evolves, law enforcement is discovering new uses for drones. Artificial intelligence is adding new abilities to drones that allow the drones to make decisions based on programming. One area of artificial intelligence that is already being implemented is facial recognition. Facial recognition allows police to use cameras and video recorders on drones to perform real-time scans of crowds and search the faces for potential matches to known suspects in their databases. If a connection is made, officers can then apprehend the person. Similarly, drones can be used to search crowds for missing people. Programmers can upload a photo of the missing person to the drone software and then use this image when scanning large crowds to see whether the image matches a face.

Such capabilities raise concerns about violation of privacy and illegal surveillance. Governments and citizens must address these issues soon because advances in drone capabilities are occurring rapidly. Furthermore, drones will likely remain a part of law enforcement as more departments recognize the advantages drones offer in reducing crime and keeping officers out of danger.

CHAPTER 3

Border Use

A group of men rush to load a truck with illegal drugs in Mexico. They intend to drive across the border into the United States. However, they do not realize that they are being captured on video by a drone 20,000 feet (6,096 m) above. The drone relays the information to operators at one of the stations run by US Customs and Border Protection (CBP), which is an agency of the US Department of Homeland Security (DHS). These officers then let ground operations know the path the truck will take, and CBP agents intercept the men once they have crossed the border. This is one of many instances of how federal agencies use drones at US borders.

CBP operations along the border of the United States and Mexico are taking advantage of drones to help maintain law and order. The US-Mexico border stretches almost 2,000 miles (3,219 km), but only an estimated one-third of it has physical barriers to deter illegal immigration and drug smuggling. The rest of the border is open terrain that is difficult to monitor. As a result, the government uses drones to assist in patrolling the vast stretches of borderlands to apprehend drug smugglers and spot anyone illegally entering the country.

Types of Drones at the Border

Depending on the mission, different types of drones are used to patrol the border. Bigger drones are able to stay aloft for some time and survey large tracts of land. They

are helpful in patrolling open desert regions and mountainous and rocky areas that would be difficult to cover on foot. Since 2006 the CBP has used Predator B drones, which are 36 feet (11 m) long and nearly 5,000 pounds (2,268 kg), to do these jobs. Predators are able to stay in the air for thirty hours at a time and have cameras that can read a license plate from 2 miles (3.2 km) above. These fixed-wing drones require a large area for takeoff and landing, so they must be launched from a command center. At the command center a drone crew, consisting of a pilot, a sensor operator, and a radar operator, controls the aircraft and relays information to CBP agents in the field.

The CBP has also begun to employ smaller drones that can be launched from anywhere, at any time, without needing runways or launch devices. In September 2017 the CBP began implementing smaller hand-launched drones such as AeroVironment's Raven and Puma. In 2018 the agency placed an order for around one hundred additional smaller drones, including about forty Aeryon SkyRaiders and sixty Lockheed Martin Indago 3 drones. These lighter drones can only fly for a few hours in fair weather, but they can be deployed quickly and near trouble spots. For this reason, these drones are used on the border for on-demand surveillance needs, such as following a certain person or car or giving a bird's-eye view of a specific area.

According to the 2018 DHS Office of Inspector General's report, in 2017 the Predators along all borders flew 5,265 hours during 635 missions. Overall, from 2011 to 2016, DHS drones flew a total of 31,000 hours, of which 20,191 were spent patrolling the southern border of the United States.

Drug-Smuggling Deterrent

A major mission of the CBP is to stop drugs from being smuggled across the border into the United States. According to a 2017 Government Accountability Office report, the CBP's drones at all borders were responsible for assisting with the agency's apprehension of more than 9,000 pounds (4,082 kg) of cocaine and more than 223,000 pounds (101,151 kg) of marijuana from 2013 to 2016. Additionally, the drone program, according to the report, helped the CBP with eight thousand specific apprehensions of drug smugglers during that time.

apprehension
a legal seizure of illegal items or an arrest

Aviation enforcement agent Dan Buress is part of the crew at the CBP's Air and Marine Operations facility in San Angelo, Texas. From there, Buress and other agents operate drones that are used five days a week to survey hundreds of miles of the southern border. The drones can be in the air for as long as eighteen hours at a time. Buress operates drones by remote control and views what the drone "sees" in real time. The cameras on the drones can identify the make and model of a car 2 miles (3.2 km) away and can stealthily follow the car as it moves. Additionally, these drones are equipped with radar, a detection system that uses radio waves to determine the location and speed of surrounding objects, and the drones relay this information to the control center. At the control center, operators consider the speed and location of the objects to help them determine whether the objects are animals, cars, or people. Using that information, the operators decide whether to investigate further.

radar
A detection system that uses radio waves to determine the location and speed of objects

These drones have caught amazing footage of smuggling efforts. One drone camera spotted a drug smuggler in Mexico using a hang glider near the border to drop 200 pounds (91 kg) of marijuana on the US side. Another video showed a sport utility vehicle packed with drugs driving up and over a portion of border wall where smugglers had built a ramp to allow access to the United States. Operators also viewed six Mexicans filling a cannon with drugs and then shooting them across the border. When these illegal activities are detected, drone operators alert officers on the ground to stop the illegal activity, seize all illicit substances, and make arrests. Troy Meridith, director of Air and Marine Operations at the facility in San Angelo, Texas, describes the strategic relationship with ground forces as productive but never-ending. "We detect and locate. They put their ground forces or Air and Marine forces out tactically," Meridith says. "They keep working and we keep going and we keep finding more and more and more."[12] Because of the successes drones have had in stopping drug smuggling, the CBP hopes to increase the number of drones deployed along the southern border.

illicit
Unlawful

Undocumented Immigrants

Another mission of the CBP is to stop people from illegally crossing the border and becoming undocumented immigrants, people who live in a country illegally. After being elected US president in 2016, Donald Trump worked to achieve his goal to build a wall that extends along the border with Mexico to stop people from crossing into the United States illegally. However, some believe there are downsides to a physical wall and think that a virtual wall, one that uses technology such as drones, makes more sense. "We can literally do technology for pennies on the dollar as compared to a physical wall," says Senator Jon Tester of Montana. Tester visited the border in 2019 and met with families who lived and farmed in the area. According to Tester, these individuals were worried about their businesses and farms being destroyed by a physical barrier. "This is about truly securing the southern border without ripping farms apart, without creating a zone that people won't be able to utilize,"[13] says Tester.

Northern Border

While most CBP drones are used to patrol the southern US border, some are also used at the northern border with Canada. The US-Canada border is actually about twice as long as the southern border, but it is not the focus of crime prevention efforts. Undocumented immigration, for example, is not a major problem along the northern border. However, FBI reports revealed by the online news source the Daily Beast in 2017 indicate that many smugglers of opioid drugs have taken advantage of the lax security along the northern border. For this reason, the US government has increased Predator drones, which first began patrolling here in 2008, along this border. Because much of the border runs along rugged terrain, many see the drones as a convenient method of surveillance. The CBP uses Grand Forks, North Dakota, as a base for Predator drones that patrol the border from Seattle, Washington, to the Great Lakes.

As the debate about a physical wall continues, the CBP has already adopted drones to help stop immigrants from crossing the US-Mexico border. CBP officers patrol the border in vehicles and on foot, but they also employ stationary cameras, stationary sensors, and now drones to monitor the border. In fact, from October 2018 to April 2019, the CBP flew drones for a total of roughly 176 flight hours along the border. During this time, because of the information drones provided, the CBP apprehended 474 individuals attempting to cross the border illegally.

One way that drones are useful is for checking out sensor hits. Along parts of the border with Mexico, there are underground seismic sensors. These sensors detect the motion of something—perhaps a person or vehicle—crossing the border. In some areas of the border, if a sensor goes off, patrols will choose to send a drone to check it out. This is because checking out every sensor hit, particularly over bad roads, can take a patrol agent hours. For example, there is a border area that runs 80 miles (129 km) be-

Border Patrol agents on the ground use information provided by drones to apprehend illegal immigrants.

VADER-Equipped Predators

Predator drones used along the southern border are typically equipped with a specialized radar called Vehicle and Dismount Exploitation Radar, or VADER. This radar was first used to help track insurgents, those fighting against the civil authority, by the US military in Afghanistan. Since then, VADER has assisted CBP agents as they track those illegally crossing the US-Mexico border. VADER is a specific radar that gives the Predator drone the ability track individuals or vehicles over a wide area and follow them as they move. From the Predator, the VADER system sends signals to ground stations that show the tracked person or object as a moving dot so that agents can easily follow its movement. VADER can even differentiate between humans, vehicles, and animals. This system is what has made drones effective at allowing agents to disrupt smuggling and illegal crossings.

tween the Arizona towns of Nogales and Lukeville. In this rugged desert region, there is no fence and a limited number of roads. If a sensor goes off, even if only a few miles away from a patrol station, it can take an agent an hour or more to reach that location. A drone, on the other hand, can get there in minutes. Sending a drone can quickly let the agents know if the sensor was hit by a person or animal. "It saves us time. It is a lot quicker to deploy this and fly it down two miles to the border, than us trying to drive it,"[14] border patrol agent Jason Weatherby says.

Drones Chasing Drones

The CBP also uses drones to stop other drones from being used in illegal activities along the border. Drug smugglers and those trying to cross the border illegally are using drone technology to help them outwit US patrols. To combat this, the CBP is using its own drones to intercept the illegal drones.

Many of the drones flown from the Mexican side of the border are used to scope out areas where the border is not being patrolled. Then drug smugglers or illegal immigrants attempt to cross at those points. Some drones are even used to carry illegal goods across the border. In January 2017 border patrol agents arrested a man who flew a drone over the checkpoint between Tijuana, Mexico, and San Diego, California. I lis drone was carrying a plastic bag packed with 13 pounds (6 kg) of methamphetamine. The *Washington Post* reported in November 2018 that over a four-day period, border patrol agents sighted thirteen drones that they suspected were carrying drugs across a section of the US-Mexico border.

The CBP uses its own drones to survey these areas for other illegal drones. If a suspicious drone lands, ground forces are sent to the location to seize it. Beyond surveillance, the CBP uses its drones to electronically take down the other drones. In 2019 the government awarded a $1.2 million contract to obtain six of Citadel Defense Company's Titan V3 drones for border use. This drone is a 20-pound (9.1 kg) device that can send signals through

Drug smugglers occasionally use drones to carry contraband across the US–Mexico border. In such cases, the CPB deploys its own drones to intercept those used by the smugglers.

the airwaves that will force the other drones to land or return to where they came from—and, according to manufacturer tests, without impacting surrounding communication systems. The border patrol agents now have these countermeasure drones as part of their arsenal to deter inappropriate border crossings by other drones.

countermeasure

an action taken against a threat

Downsides to Drone Use

While many within the government praise the use of drones along the border, others point out some negatives. One issue is weather. In 2016 the CBP conducted only 69 percent of its scheduled drone flights at the southern border. Twenty percent of the flights were canceled due to weather. Even when the flights took place, weather impacted the performance of the drones. For example, clouds hampered surveillance because the operators could not receive clear images.

Another issue is the high cost of drones. The Cato Institute, a think tank in Washington, DC, reported that Predator B drones cost $17 million to purchase and then $12,255 per flight hour to operate. Also, 18 percent of CBP drones have crashed in their first ten years, resulting in a loss of money spent. Taking all of these factors into consideration, the apprehension of a smuggler or illegal immigrant costs the federal government about $32,000 when using a drone. This cost is much higher than the $9,000 cost of apprehension using more traditional methods. "It really doesn't feel like Customs and Border Protection has a good handle on how it is using its drones, how much it costs to operate the drones, where that money is coming from or whether it is meeting any of its performance metrics,"[15] says Jennifer Lynch, a lawyer for the privacy and digital rights group Electronic Frontier Foundation. The government has to weigh these downsides when deciding the level of drone use along the border.

Future Uses

Even with the limitations of drones, the government anticipates the continued use of drones to protect the southern border. It is currently investigating new ways that drones can assist the CBP. For one, the CBP is planning to test using portable drones, drones that are small enough to launch from the back of a truck. One benefit of this type of drone is that a patrol agent could launch it while in the field, if the agent knew of a potential issue occurring in the drone's range.

Another technology being considered is facial recognition technology. The government has expressed an interest in acquiring drones with this capability. Facial recognition would allow drones to scan faces and compare images to those in the DHS database, which contains more than 170 million fingerprints and facial photos of noncitizens as they entered the United States. A drone could potentially "read" a face, compare it to those in the database, and determine whether the person has committed a crime in the past. Agents could then use that information to respond appropriately.

With the current focus on border security, the likelihood that drone use will increase along the southern border is high. "It is now clearer, almost two decades after 9/11, that drones could have a role to play in border surveillance and counter-drug operations," says Michael Horowitz, a former US Department of Defense official who has studied drone issues. "Officials outside of the military now have a better understanding of what drones are and what they can do, so it is not surprising to see requests for their use growing within the United States government."[16]

CHAPTER 4

Drone Journalism

A mass of people filled the streets in London for the 2019 People's Vote March to demand a new vote on Brexit, the controversial plan for Great Britain to leave the European Union. Those at home watching the news saw, from above, the enormous crowds that had gathered. The BBC news service used a drone to capture the enormity of the 1 million people who turned out for the protest. The drone flew high enough to bring the crowd size into focus and even trail the march as it moved through the city. Journalism had thus found another tool to report the news.

The surveillance capability of drones has given television, magazine, and internet journalists a new way to gather news footage. Photojournalists, people who photograph, edit, and display images to tell a story, use drones to provide content for these sources. They have also found that drones can provide more extensive coverage of hard-to-reach locales or developing stories that include an element of danger. Even documentary filmmakers have started to use drones to give their stories more powerful imagery. All have found that drones add to their ability to convey real situations from new perspectives.

photojournalist

Someone who photographs, edits, and displays images in order to tell a story

Why Use Drones?

One news organization to see the benefits of drone use early on was CNN, a cable news broadcaster. The FAA gave CNN permission to start a drone program in 2015. Under this program, the network tested camera-equipped drones for news gathering and reporting purposes. In 2016 CNN officially started an unmanned aerial systems unit to get aerial shots for its reporting. At the time, the unit had two dedicated drone operators and over a dozen drones of different sizes. One of the first stories CNN used drones to help cover was the 2015 earthquake in Nepal. While filming around the Nepalese capital city, Kathmandu, journalists and photographers came upon a landslide that they could not pass. CNN launched a drone, which was able to fly over the impassable terrain, and filmed several villages on the other side that were devastated from the earthquake. In addition to using the footage in its reporting, the crew gave its information to Nepalese authorities. The authorities were able to get humanitarian aid to those trapped people. Since then the aerial unit has grown to

News reporters have begun using drones to take photos following natural disasters such as hurricanes.

forty trained and licensed drone pilots. CNN has led the way, but other news agencies are quickly following.

The landslide example demonstrates how drones can help reporters reach inaccessible or dangerous places. Reporters have lost their lives when covering natural disasters, but drones allow reporters to provide visuals of what is happening without risk. In 2017 Hurricane Irma blew inland over the Florida peninsula; its winds reached speeds greater than 100 miles per hour (161 kph). As the eye of the hurricane passed over the city of Naples and the winds calmed, photojournalist Brian Emfinger immediately launched his drone. "Five minutes later, I'm flying over these destroyed mobile homes," he says. "Fifteen minutes later, I tweet out the first picture."[17] Getting such images so immediately is one of the advantages and thrills of drone use.

Another reason news agencies use drones is to save money. Often these outlets want to film events from above, but to get aerial views, organizations previously relied on helicopters, which are expensive to rent or maintain. Today news organizations are able to get the same images with drones, making them more cost efficient. Drones are also easier to launch than a helicopter, and that can result in quicker reporting of stories.

News organizations have chosen drones such as the Phantom 4, Obsidian, and Inspire 2 for their maneuvering and ease-of-launch capabilities. These devices are quadcopters that weigh less than 15 pounds (6.8 kg), and operators have real-time views of what the drones are "seeing." Some agencies have started to use autonomous drones, like the Skydio R1. Autonomous drones operate independently, without a pilot controlling their movements. The Skydio R1 can be programmed to follow something, such as a path or person, and film as it goes. This allows reporters to monitor footage or do another task while the drone follows its programmed flight path.

Assisting Photojournalists
Photojournalists who travel around the world to photograph and report on events are finding drones especially helpful in telling

more in-depth stories. For Gail Orenstein, drones have helped her show and report on happenings in conflict areas. She has been a photographer for twenty-three years, often working in combat sites or war zones. After years of using traditional photographic and video technology, in 2016 she became an FAA-licensed drone operator to expand her professional capabilities. As a pioneer in drone journalism, she became noted in the field for her amazing aerial photos, and her work has been used by news organizations around the world, including CBS News, *Time*, and the BBC. In 2017 Orenstein became the first female civilian to get drone footage of conflict in Iraq.

Often, Orenstein uses drones to help her tell the stories of conflict-related humanitarian problems around the world. For example, she used drones to get footage of Rohingya refugees crossing the Bay of Bengal to escape genocide in Myanmar. The drones give a different perspective compared to ground footage; they can reveal problems that refugees face by showing how masses of people are forced to contend with few resources. Orenstein remarks, "I fly over refugee camps to show the conditions women are forced to survive in—two toilets and 2,000 women."[18] Orenstein now finds drones an important part of her work because they add more depth to her reporting.

US photojournalist Johnny Miller lives in Cape Town, South Africa. Unlike Orenstein, his stories focus on architecture, urban issues, and climate concerns. Using drones, he photographed South African cities and published the photos under the title *Unequal Scenes*. Some were featured in the May 13, 2019, *Time* magazine cover story on the inequality still present in South Africa. The images Miller took from above show the discrepancy between rich and poor, black and white inhabitants of South African cities. His aerial photos spotlight how wealth and color barriers still separate South Africans living in urban spaces, where spacious housing developments exist just across a highway from the crude, densely packed homes of a black township. "Miller photographs what you cannot see from the ground: extreme poverty

America from Above

In 2013 photojournalist Tomas van Houtryve traveled across the United States with a drone to photograph what typical American gathering places look like from above. The series, titled *Blue Sky Days*, includes images of picnics, weddings, and people at the park, because such gatherings have been the targets of US drone strikes in foreign countries. Van Houtryve sought to remind viewers of the human cost of these remote attacks, which take place overseas and out of sight of most Americans.

Van Houtryve explains how he took his best photographs to emphasize the human factor: "The drone has a camera and I see everything that it sees on my screen, on the ground. My favorite altitude is between four and eight stories high because you can see people's shadows and their gestures." For his compelling work, he received the 2015 Infinity Award for Photojournalism.

Quoted in Laurence Cornet, "Drone Imagery and the Future of Photojournalism," Lens Culture, 2020. www.lensculture.com.

living on the doorstep of privilege and wealth," writes the *British Journal of Photography*. "While one photograph shows a luxurious golf course backing onto a densely populated settlement of tin shelters, another juxtaposes the swimming pools and private driveways of an affluent housing complex with a neighboring township."[19] After visually conveying the problems of South Africa, Miller expanded the *Unequal Scenes* project to display similar disparities in other urban environments throughout the world—all through photographs taken from his drones.

Expanding News Reporting

As with photojournalists, television and print news organizations are finding that using drones can give more depth to their news reports. CBS News discovered this as early as 2014, when it was filming a news report on the aftermath of the Chernobyl disaster, nearly three decades after it took place. The Chernobyl Nuclear

Power Plant exploded in 1986, forcing the evacuation of the city of Pripyat, Ukraine. The radiation from the disaster shortened the lives of many citizens, and the residual levels still make the area uninhabitable. Today visitors can only be on-site for short periods of time. Filmmaker Danny Cooke was able to photograph, from the ground, the site of the disaster and the city in 2014. However, he and his director wanted to give another view of the devastation. To accomplish this, Cooke thought of using a Phantom 2 quadcopter to film the city from above. "My director, Michael, wanted to show the sense of the scale of the abandoned city, and the best way to do that is by air,"[20] Cooke explains. His footage was used as part of the overall piece on CBS that allowed people to see large sections of the abandoned city from above. Sometimes, Cooke brought the drone in close to capture a still Ferris wheel and rusted bumper cars at the local amusement park, an empty swimming pool, and abandoned gas masks on the ground, providing eerie details of the empty city that the camera—and therefore the viewer—seemingly floats through.

Publishers of print news such as the *American-Statesman* newspaper of Austin, Texas, have also recognized the value of drones. By 2019 the paper had conducted more than four hundred drone launches. These launches covered everything from entertainment pieces such as cook-offs to serious stories such as Hurricane Harvey. Similarly, the Texas newspaper *Corpus Christi Caller-Times* started its drone program in early 2017. *Caller-Times* drone teams have covered potentially dangerous events such as Corpus Christi firefighters battling a fire at a grain terminal. Drones are becoming a normal part of news organizations like these throughout the United States.

Documentaries

To capture everything from the grandeur of nature to the emotion of a human-interest narrative, documentary filmmakers now film parts of their motion pictures with drones. For the documentary

Drone Schools

At certain colleges and universities in the United States, journalism students can attend classes to learn how to fly drones. They also learn drone operation safety, the legal and ethical issues of drone journalism, and the field's best practices. As drones become an integral part of journalism, these colleges and universities have started classes focusing on drone journalism. In 2012 University of Nebraska–Lincoln College of Journalism and Mass Communications professor Matthew Waite launched the Drone Journalism Lab, a program that teaches journalism students about the use of drones in their field. Since its launch, many students have taken the course, and it has now expanded to help newsrooms get started using drones for journalism by creating the *Drone Journalism Lab Operations Manual*, a guide that covers everything from preflight checklists to ethical considerations of drone journalism. Newsrooms starting drone use can employ this manual to guide them through the best methods for using drones and how to follow the laws.

Free Solo, codirector Jimmy Chin and his camera crew followed rock climber Alex Honnold up Yosemite National Park's El Capitan. Honnold used no ropes or safety gear in his ascent, making for an exciting yet perilous climb. Drones were used to show his progress. The bird's-eye view emphasized how dangerous the climb was by showing how far he was from the ground. The aerial shots also caught close-ups of him to show the level of effort it took him to make the climb. Reviews marveled at the athletic feats but also at the filmmaking techniques on display.

Nature documentary filmmakers have also discovered how effective drones can be at capturing footage. *Planet Earth II* is a 2016 British nature documentary series that was produced by the BBC. Michael J. Sanderson, a cinematographer and drone operator, worked on an episode that was set in the Amazon. There the crew used drones to observe monkeys in the inaccessible tree canopy and follow a newly discovered species, the

perilous
Dangerous or risky

Drones are now being used to capture images of wild animals in habitats that are inaccessible to human photographers.

Araguaian river dolphin, along the waterways. "I filmed the spider monkey sequence and the aerials for the river dolphins, both in the 'Jungles' episode. I mainly flew the drone over the dolphins. I got some stunning shots and behavior of this new species,"[21] Sanderson says. The surveillance capabilities of drones allowed the crew to get several different views of their subjects, making for more interesting and varied shots of creatures in their natural habitats.

Barriers to Drone Journalism

While drone journalism is providing new avenues for reporting events in the world, there are barriers to actually using drones. For one, the types of drones commonly used in journalism do not have a long battery life. Most can only fly twenty minutes at time. Additionally, they are affected negatively by weather and must be flown on relatively clear days.

Government regulations also limit drone use. In 2016 the FAA released rules on commercial drone usage, which includes media use. News agencies and other commercial groups do not need their operators to get a pilot's license as long as the drone is less than 55 pounds (25 kg), flown within eyesight by an operator with a Remote Pilot Certificate, and operated under an altitude of 400 feet (122 m). Businesses can apply for a waiver of these restrictions, but the waivers are not guaranteed.

waiver

A written agreement that allows a company or organization the right to ignore a certain rule or regulation

Drones used by journalists also cannot operate in restricted airspace. For instance, without approval or a waiver, pilots cannot fly drones within 5 miles (8 km) of an airport. Because there are many airports, especially near urban areas, this can make large areas off limits to journalists with drones. However, in 2019 the FAA expanded a program that permits drone pilots to apply to fly in these restricted spaces. The Low Altitude

Authorization and Notification Capability (LAANC) is a program meant to increase access for drone pilots to controlled airspace. Approximately six hundred airports are now covered by LAANC, and drone pilots near these areas can apply for the waivers.

Even with the limits, drone use by the media is likely to become more common in the near future. Matthew Waite, director of the Nebraska drone journalism program at the University of Nebraska–Lincoln, believes drones will become a normal part of journalism in the next few decades. "In 15 years, the things [unmanned aerial vehicles] will be used for will be boring," Waite predicts. "We'll have four or five of them sitting on the roof of the local news organization. A scanner call will go out for a bad accident and instead of sending a reporter to drive out and see if it's anything they'll just fly over it, snap a picture and make a decision."[22] Such comments suggest that drones will move from merely covering news to helping determine what is newsworthy.

CHAPTER 5

Privacy Issues

Michele Dunn lives on the third floor in a high-rise building in Atlanta, Georgia. One morning she stepped out of her shower, wrapped herself in a towel, and walked into her bedroom. Her curtains were not closed because she knew people could not see in the windows that were so high off the ground. That is when she screamed. "That's when I saw the drone," says Dunn. She stared at the device hovering outside her window. "It was so close, you could see the camera moving,"[23] she says. Her husband raced into the room and opened the window, and the drone flew away.

Dunn never found out where the drone came from, but with drone use on the rise throughout the United States, similar incidents have occurred. The FAA estimates that by 2020 there were more than 638,000 commercial drones operating in the United States, which is up from 277,000 in 2018. Over nine hundred public safety agencies have acquired drones for everything from inspections of public buildings to checking roofs, surveillance, search and rescue, and firefighting. Between the rising use of private, commercial, and government drones, individual privacy has become a hotly debated issue. Many people are concerned that drones are capturing their lives on camera without permission or notice.

Current Laws in the United States

For safety and privacy reasons, there are laws regulating the use of drones in the United States. All drones must be registered with the FAA, whether the drone is used commercially

or for personal use. Recreational drones must weigh less than 55 pounds (125 kg), can only be flown at altitudes below 400 feet (122 m), and must be in sight of their operators during flight. Commercial drone operators must obtain a Remote Pilot Certificate, which requires passing a test and a security screening. These operators cannot fly their drones at night, may not fly them outside of Class G airspace (airspace designated by the FAA as safe for flying), must keep the drone within sight, and may not fly them above people. However, commercial operators can apply for and obtain Part 107 waivers to overcome some of those restrictions.

Although the FAA regulates drone operations across the country, it does not oversee how drones are used to gather information on people or property. These rules are left up to individual states or municipalities. Many states have created laws protecting people's privacy from drones. California, for example, prohibits the use of drones to capture

municipalities

Cities or towns that have corporate status and local government video or sound recordings of another person without that person's consent. In Florida, drones may not be used for surveillance if it violates a person's reasonable expectation of privacy—this law even applies to law enforcement drones. Tennessee law prohibits the use of drones to take photos or videos at ticketed open-air events where one hundred or more people are gathered. Many of these types of laws were passed in response to complaints or concerns about drones showing up unannounced on private property or at events when privacy might be assumed.

Journalism Concerns

Celebrity wedding planner JoAnn Gregoli often sees journalist drones invade her customers' privacy. Celebrity magazines send drones in the air to photograph events that their reporters are not invited to. "These magazines are buying drones. They are able to launch them, hover them low," Gregoli explains. "You could drop a drone outfitted with video cameras into a property almost undetected. At one event I did recently in the Hamptons, one came in over the water. There is no way we could have stopped it."[24] Despite the fact it is illegal to fly over people for commercial use, some journalists ignore the laws because the pay for such exclusive photos is worth the risk involved.

Because of experiences like Gregoli's, some states have made strict drone laws concerning privacy. However, journalists argue that the laws often make it difficult to provide full coverage of news events. In Texas the laws criminalize piloting a drone less than 400 feet (122 m) above facilities such as sports arenas, jails and prisons, oil and gas drilling sites, and petroleum refineries. Since the FAA requires drones to fly below 400 feet, the Texas law makes it legally impossible to fly drones around these facilities. These types of facilities are often at the center of news stories, and journalists want—and believe the public has a right to see— photographs or videos when the situation demands them. *San Antonio Express-News* journalist Guillermo Calzada discovered the restrictiveness of the Texas law when he tried to get pictures at a deadly arson fire in San Marcos, Texas. As he flew his drone, two police officers told him he could be held criminally liable if he did not stop operating it illegally or if he published the footage he had already taken.

Because of this law, Calzada and other journalists in Texas filed a lawsuit on September 27, 2019, against the state government. The case argues that Texas's drone laws violate the First and Fourteenth Amendment rights of journalists in the state. Michael Hill, founder and chief executive officer (CEO) of Dallas-based Cumulus Technologies, a commercial drone company, insists that Texas has simply not recognized the advantages of loosening these laws and that the state will profit once they are overturned. "Texas is like way behind," says Hill. "What I tell people is Texas is the sleeping dog on the porch, and now that this dog has woken up, it's going to be the innovator in this industry. There are opportunities out there for people to start businesses . . . to help flourish and grow this industry."[25]

As issues like these occur across states, larger news agencies have taken steps to increase their ability to use drones. Because its news stories often rely on footage of crowds or events of interest, CNN obtained a waiver from the FAA in 2018 that allows the network to fly its Vantage Robotics Snap drones at an altitude of 150 feet (46 m) above ground level over open-air assemblies of people. Because of this, CNN can use drones to help cover news relating to large public events. However, CNN must still follow state and local rules wherever its drones fly, and these might restrict the filming of these events.

Controversies Along the Border

Privacy issues regarding drone use are not restricted to journalists hunting news stories. Citizens in areas where government drones operate also fear being monitored from above. For example, the CBP can operate drones within 25 to 60 miles (40 to 97 km) of the southern US border to watch for breaches of border security. Along the northern border with Canada, the CBP can operate drones

Drone Countermeasures for Sale

Concerned for privacy, some homeowners are turning to companies that offer drone countermeasures. DroneShield is a company that is based in Sydney, Australia, and has an office in Warrenton, Virginia. It makes equipment that can defeat a drone and take it down to the ground, but that is for military operations and cannot be sold to private citizens. Instead, everyday people can purchase the company's drone-detection products. These include products that can point out the location of a drone and its operator, which homeowners could use to potentially sue the operator for unauthorized use on their property. The company receives requests for these products from people such as "a VIP customer living on a compound who faces privacy threats—journalists with cameras," says Oleg Vornik, CEO of DroneShield.

Quoted in Katy McLaughlin, "The Next Big Privacy Concern Is Up in the Air," *Wall Street Journal*, June 20, 2019. www.wsj.com.

within 100 miles (161 km) of the border. As a result, more than 200 million Americans, or nearly two-thirds of the US population, can legally be filmed at any time, according to an American Civil Liberties Union (ACLU) estimate. For example, much of Maine is within the border zone, leaving its population unprotected from government surveillance. This means citizens and their homes may be filmed even if they are not the target of any investigation. Some believe this mandate to watch the border provides the government with an excuse to monitor anyone. "You'll be out gardening or sitting out enjoying the sunset, then this stupid flying lawnmower buzzes you for an hour,"[26] says Ian Finley, a Patagonia, Arizona, resident, referring to the drones that pass by his home.

With the abilities of drones to take photographs and videos of small details on the ground and of databases to store these images forever, it is not just annoying to many residents. They are worried about the possibility that they or their property are being filmed without permission. "The whole drone thing is a real threat to privacy," says Patagonia resident Clint Trafton. He is concerned about the idea of a drone "spying in your window without any kind of warrant, without anything to justify that."[27]

Currently, federal law does not require the CBP to obtain a warrant if using a drone for surveillance. In 1989 the US Supreme Court upheld warrantless aerial surveillance in the *Florida v. Riley* case. The Supreme Court ruled that there is no right to privacy when it comes to police observation in public airspace. For those living on the border, this means that they can be recorded without their consent, and this information can be shared with other government agencies. Another issue of concern is that the CBP has considered using drones with facial recognition, adding to privacy fears of residents. Additionally, the CBP will use its drones for missions assisting local law enforcement. The Cato Institute, a public policy research institution, has recommended that stricter laws regarding privacy be implemented at the border and that the CBP follow state laws if assisting local law enforcement, but to date, few changes have occurred.

The use of drones for surveillance by various government agencies concerns individuals worried about privacy.

Protest, No Pictures

In 2018 law enforcement supported a bill in Illinois that would have allowed police to use surveillance drones to monitor peaceful protests without a warrant. The bill also would have allowed police to use facial recognition technology to identify individual demonstrators photographed by drones. If the bill had passed, law enforcement would have been able to capture photos of people who were not even suspected of wrongdoing. Several civil rights groups fought against this bill. Karen Sheley, director of the ACLU Police Practices Project, said, "This is too much unchecked power to give to the police—in Chicago or anywhere." After much pushback from groups, the Illinois House of Representatives rejected the bill, but only by a narrow margin.

Quoted in Shaid Buttar, "Illinois Declines to Adopt Proposed Arbitrary Drone Surveillance of Protests," Electronic Frontier Foundation, June 22, 2018. www.eff.org.

Safety Versus Privacy

While the CBP is not bound by warrants, as of 2019 one-third of states had laws that require law enforcement to acquire warrants for drones to survey people or places. Several states are still considering warrant laws, while others have decided against them. For the states that do not require warrants, their governments claim that getting a warrant for a drone is an unnecessary step and is an obstacle to safety. California is one of these states. A bill was passed to require warrants in 2014, but then-governor Jerry Brown vetoed it. He and others in law enforcement point to their success with drones. For example, in 2019 a SWAT team in Campbell, California, deployed a new drone called the US-1 during a standoff with a suspect at a Denny's restaurant. The drone, which is equipped with thermal and optical sensors, surveyed the outside of the restaurant, including the roof and exits. In that case, police ended up using tear gas to force the suspect out of hiding. Going to a judge to get a warrant would not have allowed the team to immediately deploy a drone and resolve the situation

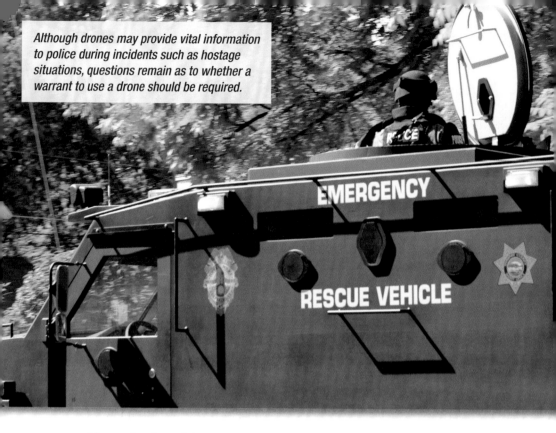

without further risk to the populace or the officers on the scene. Others point to an incident in which the Indiana police did not have time to obtain a search warrant before taking pictures of a crash site, since they needed to restore traffic flow. They used a drone to get pictures to establish who was at fault in the crash, but because it was done without a warrant, the pictures were ruled inadmissible as evidence in court.

However, critics point out that when drones are used in public, people other than the subject can have their lives recorded or photographed. Current Indiana law requires a warrant for police surveillance by drones, but in 2019 a bill was being considered to allow officers to use drones without a search warrant. "It may sound like it's a reasonable use of technology to have a drone over a public street," says Stan Wruble, a criminal defense attorney in South Bend, Indiana. "However, over a public street you can obviously look into people's backyards, you can look into people's garage areas and if you have a reasonable expectation of privacy in those areas, this sort of turns into the big brother Orwellian nightmare scenario."[28] The bill passed the Indiana House and Senate after it was amended to allow drone use without a warrant only over public events, such as emergency scenes, where there is no reasonable expectation of privacy.

Finding a Balance

Tied to worries about law enforcement taking unauthorized pictures and videos, people are concerned that their data is being stored by government agencies. For many, these concerns are warranted by the fact the videos and photos collected by border drones have not been properly protected by the government. For example, the drone program for border security information collects data from its drones, such as photos and videos, which is shared on a database used by government agencies. A 2018 report by the DHS Office of Inspector General states that the CBP has not ensured effective safeguards for information collected on and transmitted from its drones. The report states that the CBP claimed to be unaware of the protections it was supposed to follow. This leads people to be concerned about videos and images collected by other government agencies using drones. With license plate readers and facial technology poised to be used by drones, the fear of misuse will rise and need to be addressed in the courts and in the halls of government. According to a West Lebanon, New Hampshire, editorial, "With drones, as with other new technology, regulators and lawmakers ought to ask themselves this question: How could this technology be perverted to its worst possible end use?"[29] Answering this question and creating protections based on the answer will be necessary in order to strike a balance between protecting individuals' rights and allowing for greater use of an often helpful technology.

SOURCE NOTES

Introduction: Tools of Surveillance and Security

1. Quoted in *Wired*, "A Single Drone Helped Mexican Police Drop Crime 10 Percent," June 11, 2018. www.wired.com.
2. Quoted in CNN Wire, "Drone Finds Missing 6-Year-Old Boy in Cornfield Using Thermal Imaging," WTKR, October 16, 2019. https://wtkr.com.
3. Quoted in JDUNN, "Drones Show High Promise for Assisting Law Enforcement," *North Bay (CA) Business Journal*, September 29, 2014. www.northbaybusinessjournal.com.

Chapter 1: Search and Rescue

4. Quoted in Astrid Galvin, "Missing Hikers: Grand Canyon Deploys Drone Fleet in Desperate Search," *San Jose (CA) Mercury News*, April 21, 2017. www.mercurynews.com.
5. Quoted in James Willoughby, "Drones Are 'Invaluable Tool' for Scotland's Busiest Mountain-Rescue Team," *HeliGuy* (blog), November 20, 2018. www.heliguy.com.
6. Quoted in Jason Oliveiera, "Drones Helping to Fight Wildfires in California," ABC7 News, August 3, 2018. https://abc7news.com.
7. Quoted in DJI, "Drones Help Search and Rescue Teams Find Victims Faster, New Study Shows," September 20, 2018. www.dji.com.

Chapter 2: Law Enforcement

8. Quoted in Marc Nathanson, "Texas Police Use Drone to Nab Burglary Suspect," ABC News, December 6, 2019. https://abcnews.go.com.
9. Quoted in Nathanson, "Texas Police Use Drone to Nab Burglary Suspect."
10. Quoted in Vidi Nene, "London's Metropolitan Police to Use Drones for Traffic Monitoring," Drone Below, July 10, 2019. https://dronebelow.com.

11. Quoted in Haley Samsel, "How Police Forces Are Using Drones to Keep Officers Out of the Line of Fire," Security Today, July 25, 2019. https://securitytoday.com.

Chapter 3: Border Use

12. Quoted in Joce Sterman and Alex Brauer, "A Rare Look Inside the Unmanned Aircraft Program Helping to Secure Our Nation's Borders," WJLA, October 7, 2019. https://wjla.com.
13. Quoted in Shirin Ghaffary, "The 'Smarter' Wall: How Drones, Sensors, and AI Are Patrolling the Border," Vox, May 16, 2019. www.vox.com.
14. Quoted in Fox News, "Border Patrol Testing Drones to Be Its 'Eye in the Sky,'" January 19, 2018. www.foxnews.com.
15. Quoted in Brian Bennett, "Border Drones Are Ineffective, Badly Managed, Too Expensive, Official Says," Los Angeles Times, January 7, 2015. www.latimes.com.
16. Quoted in Kelsey Atherton, "The Pentagon Is Flying More Drone Missions Along the Border," Defense News, February 10, 2019. www.defensenews.com.

Chapter 4: Drone Journalism

17. Quoted in Josh Benson, "When Disasters Strike, Drones Go Where People Can't," Poynter Institute, December 13, 2017. www.poynter.org.
18. Quoted in The Guardian (Manchester), "I Believe I Can Fly: Meet the Women Drone Pilots," November 22, 2018. www.the guardian.com.
19. Quoted in British Journal of Photography, "Unequal Scenes: A New Perspective on a New Problem," November 20, 2017. www.bjp-online.com.
20. Quoted in New Current, "TNC Classic Interview," 2020. www.thenewcurrent.co.uk.
21. Quoted in Steven Flynn, "Drones in Planet Earth II: Interview with Wildlife Filmmaker Michael Sanderson," Skytango, May 2, 2017. https://skytango.com.
22. Quoted in Reporters Committee for Freedom of the Press, "Drone Journalism Begins Slow Take Off." www.rcfp.org.

Chapter 5: Privacy Issues

23. Quoted in Katy McLaughlin, "The Next Big Privacy Concern Is Up in the Air," *Wall Street Journal*, June 20, 2019. www.wsj.com.
24. Quoted in Megan Garber, "When the Wedding Crasher Is a Drone," *Atlantic*, September 30, 2015. www.theatlantic.com.
25. Quoted in Kevin Cummings, "Texas Press Association Sues State over Drone Laws," *Austin (TX) Business Journal*, October 1, 2019. www.bizjournals.com.
26. Quoted in Tim Steller, "With More Aerial Drones, Our Privacy in Border Region Is Up in the Air," *Arizona Daily Star* (Tucson, AZ), April 28, 2013. https://tucson.com.
27. Quoted in Steller, "With More Aerial Drones, Our Privacy in Border Region Is Up in the Air."
28. Quoted in David Williams, "Indiana Lawmakers Back Police Drones Without Search Warrants," WISH TV, February 13, 2019. www.wishtv.com.
29. *West Lebanon (NH) Valley News*, "Editorial: Once Again, Technology Outpaces the Law and Privacy Is the Victim," October 2, 2019. www.vnews.com.

FOR FURTHER RESEARCH

Books

Tracy Abell, *All About Drones*. Mendota Heights, MN: Focus Readers, 2017.

Sophia Barrett, *Drones in the U.S.* Hauppauge, NY: Nova Science, 2016.

John Hakala, *How Drones Will Impact Society*. San Diego, CA: ReferencePoint, 2019.

Stuart A. Kallen, *What Is the Future of Drones?* San Diego, CA: ReferencePoint, 2017.

Laura La Bella, *Drones and Law Enforcement*. New York: Rosen, 2017.

Internet Sources

Electronic Privacy Information Center, "Domestic Unmanned Aerial Vehicles (UAVs) and Drones." https://epic.org.

Stephanie Loder and Jeff Rubenstone, "Proposed FAA Drones Rules Prompt Industry Pushback," *Engineering News Record*, January 15, 2020. www.enr.com.

Willard Shepard, "No Drone Zones: FAA Takes Action to Protect Miami Super Bowl Crowds from Drones," NBC Miami, January 15, 2020. www.nbcmiami.com.

Today, "Drones Are Helping Replenish Areas Devastated by Wildfires," January 17, 2020. www.today.com.

Voice of San Diego, "Morning Report: Police Drones Are Up in the Air," January 7, 2020. www.voiceofsandiego.org.

Websites

Association for Unmanned Vehicle Systems International (www.auvsi.org). This is the world's largest nonprofit organization dedicated to the advancement of unmanned systems and robotics. The organization represents corporations and professionals from more than sixty countries. Its website details the latest drone innovations and uses in industry.

Commercial Drone Alliance (www.commercialdronealliance.org). This nonprofit organization supports reducing barriers, such as laws and regulations, to enable the freer use of commercial drones. It also advocates for advancing drone technology. Its website provides the latest news on drones, particularly focusing on the most up-to-date FAA regulations and their impacts.

Global Investigative Journalism Network: Drone Journalism (https://gijn.org/drone-journalism). This is an organization of journalists, and the drone journalism portion of its website provides links to several articles on drone journalism. These include information on how to use drones in journalism, where people can learn how to operate drones, and privacy considerations.

Know Before You Fly (www.knowbeforeyoufly.org). This website supports an education campaign that was founded by the Association for Unmanned Vehicle Systems International and the Academy of Model Aeronautics in partnership with the FAA. The purpose is to educate prospective users, both commercial and recreational, about how to use drones responsibly.

Nebraska Intelligent MoBile Unmanned Systems (NIMBUS) Lab (https://nimbus.unl.edu). The NIMBUS Lab is a research lab where software and systems engineering, robotics, and sensor networks are being used to develop higher-level unmanned aerial vehicles. Its website includes the different drone-related projects being researched.

INDEX

PICTURE CREDITS